AMERICAN JEWS REFLECT ON
WHY ISRAEL MATTERS TO THEM

A DREAM OF ZION

Teacher's Guide

Edited by Rabbi Jeffrey K. Salkin
*editor of A Dream of Zion:
American Jews Reflect on Why Israel Matters to Them*

JEWISH LIGHTS Publishing

A Dream of Zion:
American Jews Reflect on Why Israel Matters to Them Teacher's Guide

2008 First Printing
© 2008 by Jeffrey K. Salkin

Manufactured in the United States of America

Published by Jewish Lights Publishing
www.jewishlights.com

CONTENTS

INTRODUCTION

This teacher's guide will help you take some of the ideas presented in *A Dream of Zion: American Jews Reflect on Why Israel Matters to Them* and use them in classroom and learning settings. As anyone who has been involved in Jewish education knows, the entire subject of how to teach about Israel in American Jewish educational settings is a matter of great controversy. Part of the problem rests in the simple timelines of curricula; lesson plans that deal with current events or even current geo-political conditions get stale very rapidly. So, too, is the entire issue of how to present the reality of Israel to Diaspora students—motivation, follow-up, and the lack of compelling materials. While it is true that nothing in contemporary Jewish education succeeds better than Israel experiences (e.g., taglit birthright and various youth programs in Israel), the paradox is that teaching about Israel (rather than using the experience of Israel itself as the curriculum) is notoriously problematic.

This teacher's guide will help you contribute to the important and difficult task of teaching about Israel, especially as the Jewish State prepares to celebrate its sixtieth anniversary.

LOWER GRADES (4–6)

The kind of Israel education that is appropriate for younger children is, by necessity, simple. Children can understand that Israel is a land and country that is very special for Jews, as well as other religious groups. Depending on age and sophistication, they can learn how to recognize place names on a map of Israel; how to identify a few key historical figures; how to appreciate the special relationship that the nations of North America, but more specifically, the United States, have with Israel.

MY SECRET IDENTITIES

TIME: One Hour

GOAL

Students will be able to name the different "secret identities" that they have, and recognize that "Jewish" is one of them.

ACTIVITY

A free-flowing discussion about identity in which students will get the connection between being Jewish and being American.

INTRODUCTION

Today we are going to talk about who we are. How many of you like stories of super heroes? What is true of almost every super hero? They all have super powers. But they also have secret identities. Superman is also Clark Kent. Batman is also Bruce Wayne.

Name some other super heroes who have secret identities.

You don't need to have super powers to have a secret identity. In fact, we all have more than one identity. For example, here in this class, you are a student. To your friends, you are a friend. To your parents, you are a daughter or son. To your siblings, you are a sister or brother. To your grandparents, you are a grandchild.

How many identities do you have?

What are the roles that you play?

Now, along with those identities, you have other identities as well. For example, you are a member of the community in which you live. You are a resident of this state. You are a citizen of the United States.

What other people are you a member of besides the American people?

Teacher's Tip: *The Jewish people.*

As a member of the Jewish people, what other country do you care about?

Teacher's Tip: *Israel*

Listen to these words written by David Silverstein, a college student:

> "I have always struggled with the term 'American Jew.' Which identity comes first? Are they interconnected or separate entities?" (p. 22)

When are you "American"? What activities do you do when you are "American"?

When are you "Jewish"? What activities do you do when you are "Jewish"?

What times of the year make you feel more connected to either of these identities?

Listen to these words written more than ninety years ago by Louis D. Brandeis, one of the first Jews to ever sit on the United States Supreme Court and founder of Brandeis University, which was the first college in America to be founded by Jews:

> "There is no inconsistency between loyalty to America and loyalty to Jewry. The Jewish spirit, the product of our religion and experiences, is essentially modern and essentially American. Not since the destruction of the Temple have the Jews in spirit and in ideals been so fully in harmony with the noblest aspirations of the country in which they lived." (p. 213)

What does this statement mean?

Teacher's Tip: *There is no problem with being both American and Jewish.*

We can be loyal to America and to the Jewish people equally.

American ideals are similar to Jewish ideals.

What are some ideals that are common between Judaism and the United States?

Teacher's Tip: *Freedom*

Dignity of the individual

Ability to make personal choices

Caring for the environment

Opposing bigotry

Loyalty to your people

What are some similarities between the United States and Israel?

Teacher's Tip: *Democracy*

Founded on ideals

Declarations of independence

Investment and strength in technology

CONCLUSION

As American Jews, we are blessed with two identities that are interlocked with each other—like Legos that snap together. As we grow and continue our journey through life, we should enjoy the opportunities to appreciate both of those parts of our identities.

UPPER GRADES (9–12)

Students in the upper grades are obviously more sophisticated about Israel than younger students. They might read newspapers; they might watch the news; they might have already traveled to Israel; they might have engaged in heated debates about Israel and Israeli policies in secular school.

These sessions are not necessarily consecutive and/or dependent upon each other. With some adjustments, they could be used with adults as well.

WHAT IS MY CONNECTION TO ISRAEL?

TIME: One Hour

GOAL

The State of Israel is one part of a richly developed Jewish identity. The goal of this activity is to help students identify how Israel fits into their Jewish self-perception.

ACTIVITY

In this exercise, you will begin the process of helping students identify their "gut" feelings about Israel, and to begin the process of better understanding their connection to Israel.

INTRODUCTION

There is so much information and so many facts about the State of Israel today. And just as is true with most things, American Jews have many different ideas and even conflicting feelings about Israel. Today we are going to explore the many ways that American Jews relate to Israel, and how we can make those connections real in your lives.

Teacher's Tip: *To get your students talking, distribute copies of Hand-out 1, "Taking Israel Personally" (see p. 25). Ask students to complete each statement, then encourage students to share their responses with the class. Write their responses to these questions and statements on a chalk board, white board, or large sheets of paper that can be hung around the classroom.*

A Dream of Zion: American Jews Reflect on Why Israel Matters to Them suggests that there are several aspects of Israel connection:

- Israel is the **ancestral home** of the Jewish people and it is part of the Jewish identity.
- Israel is a **refuge** from anti-Semitism and a place where Jews can go to escape persecution and be safe.
- Israel is a part of Jewish **religious life.**
- Israel is an example to the rest of the world for how to engage in *tikkun olam,* repairing the world.

Teacher's Tip: *Be attentive to statements that fall into these categories. Show how the students' responses fit into these categories.*

CONCLUSION

The State of Israel means many different things to American Jews. Today we have begun to define our relationships with Israel.

Session II

ISRAEL: YOURS, MINE AND OURS

TIME: One Hour

GOAL

Students will be able to articulate the ways in which Jews connect to Israel.

ACTIVITY

This is an interactive values clarification activity.

Teacher's Tip: *This session works best if it follows the previous session. If this is not the case, introduce students to the aspects of Israel connection as noted in the previous activity (see p. 12).*

MATERIALS

A large room, such as a social hall

Butcher block paper or large Post-its.

Teacher's Tip: *Prior to the class, write the following phrases on the paper (one phrase per piece):*

> Ancestral home/part of my identity
>
> Refuge from anti-Semitism and a safe place for Jews
>
> Part of Jewish religious life
>
> An example to the world for how to engage in *tikkun olam*, repairing the world

Post one page in each of the four corners of the room. Distribute copies of Hand-out 2, "For Me, Israel Is …" (see pp. 26–28).

INTRODUCTION

There are many ways that American Jews relate to Israel. Who would like to share some of those ways?"

Teacher's Tip: *Solicit responses.*

Today we are going to consider at least four answers to that question. Around the four corners of the room I have put four ways that American Jews relate to Israel.

Teacher's Tip: *Read aloud to the class the four categories.*

Ask students to go to the corner that most defines their connection to Israel.

Ask students to read the quotes that illustrate that connection, and be prepared to present the quotes that are most meaningful to them in the general discussion that follows.

In what ways did your reasons for supporting Israel change as a result of what we did today?

What reasons for supporting Israel do you think are the most valid?

Which reasons will have the most lasting value for American Jews?

CONCLUSION

Despite (or even because) of our many reasons for understanding Israel, there are clear actions that can flow out of those commitments. Any relationship needs some kind of action to accompany it. Let's look at what some of those actions might be.

Teacher's Tip: *Distribute copies of Hand-out 3, "A Covenant of Relationship with Israel" (see p. 29).*

DO YOU FEEL THE LOVE?

TIME: One Hour, Thirty Minutes

GOAL

This is a lesson on how American Jews feel about Israel, and how those feelings have changed. It requires that participants become "junior sociologists" and analyze their findings. *It is necessary that it take place on a Sunday morning in the synagogue, or at a time when there would be the largest number of people at the synagogue, especially representing multiple generations. Ideally, arrange it for a day and time when there is a family education program, Sisterhood or Brotherhood/men's club, a bazaar, or other large gathering.*

ACTIVITY

Students become sociologists for a while, interviewing members of their Jewish community to discern how others feel about Israel.

INTRODUCTION

There has been a lot written recently on how American Jews feel about Israel, especially as we approach the sixtieth anniversary of Israel's founding. Today we are going to become sociologists and analyze how our own community members feel about Israel.

MATERIALS

Copies of Hand-out 4, "How Do I Feel about Israel?" (see p. 30)
Pencils

The Interviews

This portion of the activity should take 30 minutes. Distribute copies of "How Do I Feel about Israel?" sheets to students. Ask students to interview people at the synagogue about the statements on the sheets. They should record not only the person's reaction to the statements but also the age category of the interviewee.

Discussion

This portion of the activity should take 30 minutes. Reassemble students and discuss responses to each statement. Ask students for the responses within each age group. Calculate the average response to each statement for each age group.

While this experiment is clearly not a valid sociological sampling, we might have found some patterns. Are there discernable patterns according to age group?

Steven M. Cohen and Ari Kelman have done a study in which they show that younger Jews are less likely to have strong positive feelings about Israel. Why do you think that this is the case?

Rabbi Jeffrey K. Salkin, in his introduction to *A Dream of Zion: American Jews Reflect on Why Israel Matters to Them*, has suggested several reasons for this "loss of love":

- The intifadas (Palestinian uprisings) and the way that Israel has seemed to respond to them have eroded support.
- The perception that Israel is a dangerous place.
- The phenomenon of Israelis leaving Israel to live elsewhere.
- Various behaviors, incidents and policies (i.e., the separation fence) have been openly criticized.
- The religious gap between Orthodox and non-Orthodox Judaism in Israel.

What do you think of each? In your experience, what effect have these perceptions had on the way Israel itself is perceived?

Teacher's Tip: *High school students may need some prompting in this area. A highly effective way of doing this is to ask, directly: "What do your non-Jewish friends and teachers say about Israel? How does media portray Israel?" It will be crucial for you to prepare for this before hand, with newspaper clippings from local newspapers and with some sense of what is being said on television news programs.*

What are the appropriate ways to criticize Israel? What language should we use? What kinds of sentiments should we express?

How can you tell the difference between legitimate criticism of Israel's policies, anti-Israel sentiment, and anti-Semitism?

CONCLUSION

As American Jews, it is not necessary for us to always agree with Israel's policies 100 percent of the time. Israel, like any country, has its good points and its not-so-good points. But it is absolutely necessary for us to be knowledgeable about Israel and to be able to differentiate good, constructive criticism from potentially harmful criticism.

DISCUSSION GUIDE TO "FOR ME, ISRAEL IS ..."

The following quotes are from *A Dream of Zion: American Jews Reflect on Why Israel Matters to Them*, edited by Rabbi Jeffrey K. Salkin (Woodstock, VT: Jewish Lights, 2007), www.jewishlights.com.

Teacher's Tip: *If you want to use the quotes in Hand-out 2, "For Me, Israel Is ..." as teaching material, use this discussion guide. This is particularly good with adult learners, who will have the maturity, perspective, and knowledge of history and current events to engage in meaningful discussion of these issues.*

Ideas for use:

- These quotes can be used during a program celebrating Israel's sixtieth anniversary. Give copies of the hand-out to members of your community and ask them to comment on them publicly.
- These quotes can be used for sermonic material.
- These quotes can be used, with attribution, in synagogue and center bulletins as a lead-up to Israel's sixtieth anniversary in May 2008.

ANCESTRAL HOME AND PART OF MY IDENTITY

"We carry a responsibility to support Israel and to keep her strong."
—Matthew Brooks (p. 9)

Do you agree with this statement?

What are the best ways to support Israel?

What are the best ways to keep Israel strong?

"There are countries that have more beautiful museums than Israel. There are countries that have older universities than Israel. There are countries that have much more magnificent architecture and art than Israel. But Israel is like your mother."
　　—Peninnah Schram (p. 20)

What does Schram mean when she says that Israel is like your mother?

What is Schram saying about our relationship with Israel?

"Somehow, the living reality of Israel, all of its dreadful problems notwithstanding, encourages and strengthens me."
　　—Alan Mittleman (p. 40)

What kind of "dreadful problems" are there in Israel?

In what ways does Israel encourage and strengthen you?

"Israel matters—because as Jews, we share so much in common no matter on what side of the ocean we choose to make our home."
　　—Lisa D. Grant (p. 42)

What do all Jews have in common?

"It is the person who, while living outside Israel, does tangible acts to connect to the land—visiting Israel, buying Israeli products, calling friends in Israel, advocating for Israel, supporting the redemptive mission of the people of Israel in the Land of Israel. Only someone who lives in Israel is a complete Zionist, but in the exile we can constantly yearn to be there. To paraphrase Rav Nahman of Breslov, wherever I am walking I am walking to Israel."
　　—Rabbi Avraham Weiss (pp. 164–165)

What kind of tangible acts can Jews outside Israel do to show their loyalty and connection to Israel?

Which acts seem to be the most important to you?

How would you rate your community as a whole in its support of Israel?

What is your opinion of the traditional Jewish idea that those who live outside of Israel are living in exile? How relevant is this idea today?

"We Jews are not just a spiritual community—we are a people, one that will only fulfill its collective potential with a state in which we can hammer out the details."
　　　—Ariel Beery (p. 170)

In what ways are Jews a spiritual community?

In what ways are Jews a people?

What does Beery mean by "details"? What kind of "details" need to be hammered out?

ISRAEL AS A PLACE OF REFUGE

"I sleep better at night knowing there is not just the Land of Israel, but the sovereign State of Israel, the national homeland of the Jewish people."
　　　—Rabbi Nina Beth Cardin (p. 71)

What do you think Cardin meant?

What is your opinion of this statement?

What is the difference between the Land of Israel and the "sovereign State of Israel?"

"The creation of the State of Israel undoubtedly gives Jews greater dignity."
　　　—Harold Grinspoon (p. 74)

In what ways does the State of Israel give Jews greater dignity?

At what times might you have disagreed with this statement?

"Only the re-establishment of a Jewish State can effectively cure the virus of anti-Semitism, from which we Jews have suffered so grievously."
　　　—Rabbi Roland B. Gittelsohn (p. 228)

In what ways has Israel "cured" the virus of anti-Semitism? In what ways has it failed to do so?

In what ways has Israel and/or Israel's actions "created" anti-Semitism?

What is the difference between anti-Semitism, anti-Zionism, and "anti-Israelism?"

"Six decades after the founding of their state, the Jews of Israel should not have to argue for the legitimacy of their national existence. They are at home in their land by a long-established right, and they can take justifiable pride in their country's history and achievements."
  —Alvin H. Rosenfeld (p. 78)

What is the "long established right" that Rosenfeld is describing?

What aspects of Israel's history make you proud?

What aspects of Israel's achievements make you proud?

What aspects of Israel's history and/or achievements make you less than proud?

"I do not believe in a god, but I do believe I am a Jew—and therefore, what happens to Israel, happens to me."
  —Nat Hentoff (p. 79)

What are your own personal feelings about Hentoff's statement that what happens to Israel happens to him?

In what ways, if any, do you take what happens in Israel "personally?"

"I cannot imagine my life without Israel and I would not count on the survival of the Jewish people—spiritually, psychologically, or physically—without Israel."
  —Danny Maseng (p. 87)

In what ways do you agree with Maseng?

How would life be different for the Jews—spiritually, psychologically, physically—without Israel?

If there were no longer any Israel, what effect would it have on the Jewish people as a whole?

Could Israel survive as a state, though not a specifically Jewish State?

ISRAEL IS A PART OF JEWISH RELIGIOUS LIFE

"I see Israel as the place that inspires us to live in the present, to live life with all of its uncertainties and complexities, as fully and richly as possible."
  —Rabbi Bradley Hirschfield (p. 101)

In what ways does Israel inspire us to live with uncertainty and complexities?

"[Israel] reminds me that ... a people can become resurrected from its ashes."
—Rabbi Jeffrey K. Salkin (p. 108)

Do you agree with Salkins' use of the term "resurrected?"

In what ways have the Jewish people become "resurrected" through the existence of Israel?

"A basic look at the history of [the people of] Israel from ancient times until today uncovers a constant divine protection and providence."
—Rabbi Hirshy Minkowicz (p. 127)

At what times did it appear that the Jewish people lived under divine protection and guidance?

At what times was it particularly difficult to believe that statement?

"The Talmud records that from the exile a person ought to be a *doresh Tzion*, a seeker of Zion (Rosh Ha-shana 30a). For me, a *doresh Tzion* is someone who recognizes that his or her life as a Jew in the Diaspora is incomplete."
—Rabbi Avraham Weiss (p. 164)

In what ways are our Jewish lives in the Diaspora incomplete?

In what ways are our Jewish lives in the Diaspora complete?

"To survive and develop creatively, a civilization must have a locus, a laboratory or hot-house, if you will, where it can be the primary culture of its people, where new strands and strains may be tested and refined."
—Rabbi Roland B. Gittelsohn (p. 229)

If the State of Israel is a "laboratory" for Jewish life, what is being developed there?

What is being "tested and refined?"

ISRAEL IS AN EXAMPLE TO THE WORLD

"Israel is a bastion of hope in a world filled with despair."
—Dr. Marc D. Angel (p. 137)

In what ways does the State of Israel give you hope in a world filled with despair?

"The essential moral failing of Israel—its inability to deal fairly with the rights and even the full humanity of the other people with whom it shares a homeland—remains deeply troubling."
    —Rabbi Arthur Green (p. 151)

To what extent do you agree with Green?

"I dare to hope that Israel will find a way to make peace with its neighbors; that it will find a way to accomplish the very difficult task of being both a Jewish State and a democracy granting freedom of religion to all its citizens, including its Jewish ones; and that it will flourish materially, intellectually, culturally, and spiritually."
    —Rabbi Elliot N. Dorff (p. 158)

Which elements of being a Jewish State and being a democracy are inherently in conflict?

How can Jews in the Diaspora help Israel flourish materially, intellectually, culturally, and spiritually?

"I don't believe in chosen peoples and promised lands. I don't think God plays favorites or deals in real estate. But ... there are certain places on this planet that hold deep promise for personal and planetary transformation and renewal. Israel is one of these places."
    —Rabbi Rami M. Shapiro (p. 202)

What is your conception of the idea of a chosen people? A chosen land?

In what ways does Israel hold deep promise for transformation and renewal?

What other places in the world hold similar potential?

"I wonder how many of the next generation are walking away from a serious engagement with Israel, if only because we have failed to welcome, let alone encourage and invite, the expression of serious skepticism, criticism, and opposition."
    —Steven M. Cohen (p. 176)

In what ways is it wise for the Jewish community to foster criticism of Israel?

What kind of "rules" might there be for criticism of Israel?

"The Israel I love should be and *must* be an Israel of justice for all its citizens, and an Israel that believes in the power of words as its first defense before using its necessarily strong military might. That is my Judaism and it is my Zionism."

    —Peter Edelman (p. 195)

What does Edelman mean when he speaks of balancing words and military might?

Taking Israel Personally

To be used with *A Dream of Zion: American Jews Reflect on Why Israel Matters to Them*, edited by Jeffrey K. Salkin (Woodstock, VT: Jewish Lights, 2007), www.jewishlights.com.

When I hear the word "Israel," the first thing that pops into my mind is ...

When I realize that there is going to be something about Israel on the news, I feel ...

For me, Israel is ...

For most Americans, Israel is ...

I wish that Israel could be ...

When I think about visiting Israel, I ...

The best thing that I have ever heard about Israel is ...

The worst thing that I have ever heard about Israel is ...

When I hear criticisms of Israel and/or its policies, I ...

The thing about Israel that gives me the greatest amount of pride is ...

The thing that worries me about Israel is ...

For Me, Israel Is...

To be used with *A Dream of Zion: American Jews Reflect on Why Israel Matters to Them*, edited by Jeffrey K. Salkin (Woodstock, VT: Jewish Lights, 2007), www.jewishlights.com.

ANCESTRAL HOME AND PART OF MY IDENTITY

"We carry a responsibility to support Israel and to keep her strong."
        —Matthew Brooks (p. 9)

"There are countries that have more beautiful museums than Israel. There are countries that have older universities than Israel. There are countries that have much more magnificent architecture and art than Israel. But Israel is like your mother."
        —Peninnah Schram (p. 20)

"Somehow, the living reality of Israel, all of its dreadful problems notwithstanding, encourages and strengthens me."
        —Alan Mittleman (p. 40)

"Israel matters—because as Jews, we share so much in common no matter on what side of the ocean we choose to make our home."
        —Lisa D. Grant (p. 42)

"It is the person who, while living outside Israel, does tangible acts to connect to the land—visiting Israel, buying Israeli products, calling friends in Israel, advocating for Israel, supporting the redemptive mission of the people of Israel in the Land of Israel. Only someone who lives in Israel is a complete Zionist, but in the exile we can constantly yearn to be there. To paraphrase Rav Nahman of Breslov, wherever I am walking I am walking to Israel."
        —Rabbi Avraham Weiss (pp. 164–165)

"We Jews are not just a spiritual community—we are a people, one that will only fulfill its collective potential with a state in which we can hammer out the details."
        —Ariel Beery (p. 170)

ISRAEL AS A PLACE OF REFUGE

"I sleep better at night knowing there is not just the Land of Israel, but the sovereign State of Israel, the national homeland of the Jewish people."
—Rabbi Nina Beth Cardin (p. 71)

"The creation of the State of Israel undoubtedly gives Jews greater dignity."
—Harold Grinspoon (p. 74)

"Only the re-establishment of a Jewish State can effectively cure the virus of anti-Semitism, from which we Jews have suffered so grievously."
—Rabbi Roland B. Gittelsohn (p. 228)

"Six decades after the founding of their state, the Jews of Israel should not have to argue for the legitimacy of their national existence. They are at home in their land by a long-established right, and they can take justifiable pride in their country's history and achievements."
—Alvin H. Rosenfeld (p. 78)

"I do not believe in a god, but I do believe I am a Jew—and therefore, what happens to Israel, happens to me."
—Nat Hentoff (p. 79)

"I cannot imagine my life without Israel and I would not count on the survival of the Jewish people—spiritually, psychologically, or physically—without Israel."
—Danny Maseng (p. 87)

ISRAEL IS A PART OF JUDAISM

"I see Israel as the place that inspires us to live in the present, to live life with all of its uncertainties and complexities, as fully and richly as possible."
—Rabbi Bradley Hirschfield (p. 101)

"[Israel] reminds me that ... a people can become resurrected from its ashes."
—Rabbi Jeffrey K. Salkin (p. 108)

"A basic look at the history of [the people of] Israel from ancient times until today uncovers a constant divine protection and providence."
—Rabbi Hirshy Minkowicz (p. 127)

"The Talmud records that from the exile a person ought to be a *doresh Tzion*, a seeker of Zion (Rosh Ha-shana 30a). For me, a *doresh Tzion* is someone who recognizes that his or her life as a Jew in the Diaspora is incomplete."
—Rabbi Avraham Weiss (p. 164)

"To survive and develop creatively, a civilization must have a locus, a laboratory or hot-house, if you will, where it can be the primary culture of its people, where new strands and strains may be tested and refined."
—Rabbi Roland B. Gittelsohn (p. 229)

ISRAEL IS AN EXAMPLE TO THE WORLD

"Israel is a bastion of hope in a world filled with despair."
—Dr. Marc D. Angel (p. 137)

"The essential moral failing of Israel—its inability to deal fairly with the rights and even the full humanity of the other people with whom it shares a home-land—remains deeply troubling."
—Rabbi Arthur Green (p. 151)

"I dare to hope that Israel will find a way to make peace with its neighbors; that it will find a way to accomplish the very difficult task of being both a Jewish State and a democracy granting freedom of religion to all its citizens, including its Jewish ones; and that it will flourish materially, intellectually, culturally, and spiritually."
—Rabbi Elliot N. Dorff (p. 158)

"I don't believe in chosen peoples and promised lands. I don't think God plays favorites or deals in real estate. But ... there are certain places on this planet that hold deep promise for personal and planetary transformation and renewal. Israel is one of these places."
—Rabbi Rami M. Shapiro (p. 202)

"I wonder how many of the next generation are walking away from a serious engagement with Israel, if only because we have failed to welcome, let alone encourage and invite, the expression of serious skepticism, criticism, and oppo-sition."
—Steven M. Cohen (p. 176)

"The Israel I love should be and *must* be an Israel of justice for all its citizens, and an Israel that believes in the power of words as its first defense before using its necessarily strong military might. That is my Judaism and it is my Zionism."
—Peter Edelman (p. 195)

A Covenant of Relationship with Israel

What can you do to support Israel? *(Check those things that you might want to do.)*

- ❏ Visit Israel
- ❏ Make Israeli friends who live in Israel and stay in touch with them.
- ❏ Improve my knowledge of Hebrew.
- ❏ Become familiar with Israeli art.
- ❏ Follow what's happening in the Israeli sports world.
- ❏ Whenever possible, buy Israeli products, especially food products.
- ❏ Write letters to the newspaper supporting and defending Israel.
- ❏ Give *tzedakah* to organizations that support Israel. (These would include such organizations as United Jewish Communities, Jewish National Fund, the Abraham Fund, New Israel Fund, Americans for Peace Now, ARMDI [Magen David Adom, the Israeli "Red Cross"], ARZA [Association of Reform Zionists of America], the Masorti movement in Israel, just to name a few.
- ❏ Read Israeli newspapers and magazines online. (See "Suggestions for Further Reading and Sources of Current Information," pp. 255–257, in *A Dream of Zion: American Jews Reflect on Why Israel Matters to Them* for ideas.)
- ❏ Read books about Israel.
- ❏ Become aware of, and listen to, Israeli rock music.
- ❏ Rent and watch Israeli films.
- ❏ Learn to cook Israeli and Middle Eastern dishes.

Fill in your other ideas here:

How Do I Feel about Israel?

On a scale of 1 (least agreement) 2 (neutral) 3 (most agreement), what is your response to the following statements?

STATEMENT	GENERAL AGE OF RESPONDENT 15–20, 20–35, 35–45 / 55+	RANKING
Caring about Israel is a very important part of my Judaism.		
If Israel were destroyed, it would be one of the worst things in my life.		
I am a supporter of Israel.		
Sometimes I don't like what I hear about Israel.		
Israel occupies land that belongs to other people.		
Though I don't agree with terrorism, I think that the Palestinians should have their own state.		
I am uncomfortable with the idea of a "Jewish State."		

RABBI JEFFREY K. SALKIN is recognized as one of the most thoughtful Jewish writers and teachers of his generation. He has helped people find spiritual meaning in both the great and small moments in life.

A noted writer whose work has appeared in *Moment, Reform Judaism, Sh'ma,* the *Wall Street Journal, Reader's Digest,* and the *Congressional Record,* Rabbi Salkin is also the author of *Putting God on the Guest List, 3rd Ed.: How to Reclaim the Spiritual Meaning of Your Child's Bar or Bat Mitzvah; For Kids—Putting God on Your Guest List: How to Claim the Spiritual Meaning of Your Bar or Bat Mitzvah; The Bar/Bat Mitzvah Memory Book, 2nd Ed.: An Album for Treasuring the Spiritual Celebration* (with Nina Salkin); and *Being God's Partner: How to Find the Hidden Link Between Spirituality and Your Work,* with an introduction by Norman Lear (all Jewish Lights).

He has served as the co-chair of the Commission on Outreach for the Union for Reform Judaism, and has served on its board as well as on the board of the Central Conference of American Rabbis.

OTHER JEWISH LIGHTS BOOKS BY RABBI JEFFREY K. SALKIN

JEWISH LIGHTS Publishing
www.jewishlights.com